Just To See How It Feels

Just To See How It Feels

Poems by Allison Cundiff

Word Poetry

Published by Word Poetry
P.O. Box 541106
Cincinnati, OH 45254-1106

ISBN: 9781625492784

Poetry Editor: Kevin Walzer
Business Editor: Lori Jareo

Visit us on the web at www.wordpoetrybooks.com

Cover design, photography, and line art by Anthony Gaddis

For Lyla

לילה היקרה,
את נמצאת היכן שאת אמורה להיות, ולקמיל, על כל האומץ בצעירותך.

"How refreshing to learn, right up front and in the words of the poet herself, just where she is coming from. The poems reveal eloquently how the year 2016, tumultuous politically as well as personally, *felt* to her both bodily and spiritually. The year's seasons, and special moments therein, are illuminated with intimacy, intensity, and insight. What a treat." -Robert Bates Graber, author of *Valuing Useless Knowledge* and *Plutonic Sonnets*

"Allison Cundiff's poetry doesn't tell a story to the reader so much as it includes them. Her prose is a slow dance of imagery and vulnerability as huge moments are revealed through small revelations. Her voice is honest, her tone intimate, but still somehow inviting, turning strangers into close friends and confidants with each turn of the page. She refuses to shy away from the uncomfortable and unknown, instead turning to face it directly." -Marcus Eder, author of *Rorschach's Ribs*, *Holidaze*, and *Nobody Puts Swayze in the Corner*

"What I adore most about this chapbook, *Just To See How it Feels*, is the delicate balance the poet achieves between the relentless story that demands to be told and the beauty of the language she uses to tell it. This is the world where the frond becomes the infant, where women wait for husbands in the witching hour, and the old love, the original, earthly love, returns again and again as children, mothers, and lovers. Absolutely recommended." -Andrew Demcak, author of *Night Chant*

"*Just to See How it Feels* is about living life with courage, curiosity, and wide-open eyes. Sometimes, as when risking a walk on a frozen lake, we fall through, and so this book is also about redemption that takes the form of an unexpected grandchild, snapping turtle eggs, or 'the small goodness' of love. This book is not about regret, which also makes it a joy to read." -Richard Newman, author of *All the Wasted Beauty of the World* and *Graveyard of the Gods*

"The poems of Allison Cundiff's *Just To See How It Feels* are deeply scored with clear-eyed tenderness. This book is rich with poems finely wrought and wise about the choices we make, the visions we have of ourselves, and our loved ones. Keenly aware of what's at stake, where the heart is, what the moment can offer us, Cundiff's poems exhibit a raw intimacy between the poet and those loved, those lost, and those still living near." -Christopher Salerno, author of *Sun & Urn*

Table of Contents

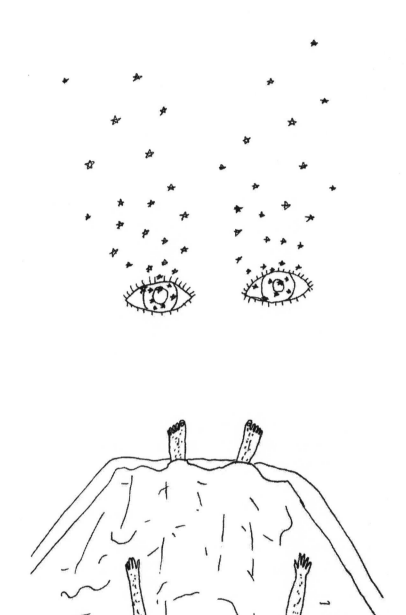

Introduction

I did not expect to become a grandmother at 40.

Newly divorced, I was working two teaching jobs, struggling to pay for my 16 year-old daughter's cello lessons. Child support was spotty, and all I could think about was keeping life as normal as possible for her.

While I immersed myself in work, my daughter worked in her little music studio, practicing the Popper etudes and her scales, well after I came home at night. I would collapse into bed, sometimes without washing off my mascara, hearing the cello's muffled sound as I fell asleep, the dark tone a sort of balm for our hectic lives.

It is that time, the time in the middle of the rushing about, that life really happens. And real life usually has nothing at all to do with our expectations or our routines.

Near the end of that December I arrived home around 8 pm, my arms holding the day's coffee gone cold and the end of term's stack of papers. My daughter was in bed, recovering still from a flu that had lingered through November. I knew she had a concert the next day and that she should be practicing.

"You alright in there? I'm home. I brought cookies from school," I called from the other room.

"Just taking a quick nap," she said, her voice muffled under the covers.

I walked into her room, turning on the light by her bed. She was lightly asleep, her forehead warm. She had this flu for what seemed like a month. The previous weekend we had friends over for dinner, and she didn't join us for pho, her favorite. She had asked for crackers around midnight, and I brought them in, a glass of wine in my hand, and sat on the edge of her bed as she nibbled, just to get sick moments later. I told her not to worry, that she'd feel better the next day. But I knew I would call her pediatrician in the morning to be sure.

The next day, we were driving home from a family event. "We need to call about getting you into the doctor," I said.

She hesitated. "Can I talk to you about something?" Her voice was small.

"Sure," I said, as I fidgeted in my purse for the phone. She put her hand on my arm to stop me.

"It's about… sex," she said.

"Okay," I said, my heart starting to beat faster.

"Well, I had it," she said, looking out the window of the car. *My God, do orchestra types have sex?* I wondered.

"You did?" She nodded. "Well, did you use protection?" I couldn't believe it. She still seemed so young to me.

"Protection, yes…"

And the next part came out in a rush. The condom, she said, had broken. And she was finally telling me after nearly two months, six pregnancy tests, many nights of crying with her boyfriend of the past year, and a failed Latin test due to a panic attack and "my God, mom I'm so sorry and scared." Her mouth was moving and as all the words came out I felt my heart twisting from the inside. All the questions stuck in my throat. *How could this happen? Why didn't she tell me until two months in? How long had she known? Is she alright? Is she going to be alright?* The guilt and worry clawed at me. I had been working too much, I should have been around more. She had been making her own dinners for Christ's sake. I was driving down the highway, and all I could think to do was reach over and take her hand and tell her, "Everything will be okay. I promise." And I think I saw, through all her tears, relief.

The next day was a blur. It began with easy things, which surprised me: a call to the doctor, prenatal vitamins, a sit down with her boyfriend and his mother, thankfully, everyone calm and rational. We decided to wait to tell anyone else. We had to get the kids taken care of first. On the couch that evening, a small pot of green tea between us, I presented Camille with her options. She knew she could terminate and had felt that pressure from some she had told before me, but she couldn't bear that. The other two options, keep the baby or adoption, were what she was struggling with. I told her what I knew of open adoptions. Her eyes became wide, "You mean, I can give the baby up and still see it?"

At three months along, the baby had grown to the length of a peapod. We had heard the heartbeat at the doctor's, my daughter and her boyfriend clasped hands on the table, their eyes frenzied with the hugeness of what was between them. After hearing that heartbeat and in between practicing Bach suites later that evening, she looked up from her cello and announced quite matter-of-factly, "Mom, I decided. I want to give the baby up for adoption." My whole body ached for her. I knew what was in front of her. The world's eyes on her body, the judgement. But she had decided, and as her mother, I was determined to cushion what was coming to the best of my ability.

That night we started looking for adoptive families. We found several websites listing people's qualification to parent. So many people who had love to offer. They had drop-down menus listing the characteristics we could choose from: gender of the parents, location in the country, ethnicity, professions. Page after page of people. I saw a couple with dark hair smiling. The woman wore a doctor's coat. IVF hadn't worked for them. There was another family in New York City, a picture of them at the MoMA. They had lost a child. We clicked the box that said OPEN as opposed to CLOSED or SEMI-OPEN adoption and the families were reduced to less than a dozen. But there was the dark-haired couple that I had liked. San Francisco, Educated. Progressive. Seeking an open adoption. I clicked on their profile.

One step in the process of selecting an adoptive family is the interviews. We had several. It felt like dating but without the flowers and candy. There was the same battery of questions: Tell us about you. What are your interests? What kind of family do you imagine for yourself? And just like walking away from a romantic nonmatch, we walked away from family nonmatches, difficult as this was. All these people seemed good. All had love to give. One of the more heart-breaking interviews we had was with a woman in Texas, 40, who feared many potential birth mothers worried she was too old to be a mother. *What about me*, I thought. *Am I not too young to be a grandmother?* But there's no luxuriating in your own concerns when your child is a pregnant junior in high school. My own baby, her color drained from morning sickness, her tiny belly swelling, was going through something I never had to understand, so the least I could be was strong.

Our phone interview with the dark-haired couple was set for the next day. They had grown up with siblings who were adopted, and the woman had been raised on a kibbutz. They spoke multiple languages in the home. While my daughter spoke with both of them, I stepped out of the room to give them space, and the weight of the past month hit me in the chest. I stopped, my hand on the wall to steady myself, grateful for the door blocking my daughter's view of me. *My God*, I thought, *this life*.

15

What am I going to do? But the dog was crying to go outside, and I had to check on dinner on the stove, and those small things made me take a deep breath and continue. One step at a time.

A teenage pregnancy proceeds much like an adult one but with small social differences. Camille's growing belly on her too-young face was a concern. She switched schools for the spring semester, keeping her story quiet, but people still talked. She stayed quiet. She practiced her cello for hours a day, her belly alive under the Elgar, the Bach. The neighbors were protective of us. The dogs knew something was up. Our beagle slept on Camille's body, cocking her head at the baby's kicks, making us laugh.

We decided on the dark-haired family to raise Camille's baby. Their names, Shahaf and Pnina, would become names we would speak in our home daily from then on, to one another, to Camille's baby inside of her. Camille approached it like she would asking out her crush from English class in the high school cafeteria.

"Would you please be the adoptive parents of my baby?" (*God, please stay close to us,* I thought).

"Yes, it would be our honor," they responded, their voices changed by the joy of it.

Camille and I visited Shahaf, Pnina, and their family that spring. Camille was very pregnant. People looked too long at her in the airport as she waddled to pick up her decaffinated coffee from Starbucks. Though healthy, she was clearly too young to be a mother. But when we arrived in San Francisco, this very beautiful, selfless, and grateful family quite normally took us into their home, and we toured the city as they demonstrated all the normal love that the baby would one day experience. One day, when parking outside a museum, Shahaf dropped us off so Camille wouldn't have to walk too far. We spent the day in a fragrant garden, talking about classical music then waited outside in the sun while Shahaf fetched the car. Some time passed and Pnina got a call. "Shahaf is upset," she said. "Traffic is terrible, and he'll be a bit." Camille shot me a glance, worried. We would see them navigate conflict. Would he holler, like Camille's father did? Would he be silent? But he pulled up, and as we got settled in the car, Pnina put her hand on Shahaf's shoulder. He said calmly, "that was frustrating. There was so much traffic!" And Camille started laughing in the backset, tears in her eyes, relieved.

Though the life I expected for myself and my daughter was broken apart that year, the pregnancy helped us recognize a strength I had no idea was inside of us. It was almost as I had to disappear completely in order to become the best, strongest version of a mother. And in the midst of the cracking apart of her expectations of what teenage life would be, my daughter became a more beautiful person. And a baby got to have a life. And a new family was born.

We all want our children to grow up to be successful. Though Camille's path was suspended a bit that year, she became successful in a different way. She showed me her absolute selflessness. It took the breaking apart of our expectations of normalcy for that to happen. Thank God for the breaking apart.

On our last day in San Francisco, as Camille was seated between Pnina and Suzi, the baby's other grandmother to be, the baby started kicking. The baby, a girl, who would be born two months later and be named Lyla Shelly, was quiet most of that visit, probably because of all of the walking. But as we parked, Camille felt her kicking. "Wait," she said suddenly, and grabbing the hand of the woman on either side of her, pulled their hands to her moving belly, saying, "Here she is. Here's your daughter."

Dear Reader:

The poems in this collection were written in response to the events described in the introduction. Though a pregnancy inspired the conflict, the themes stretch into the whole body, surprised by pain, delighted by tenderness, rubbed raw by other people's goodness and cruelty.

The subjects that produce poetry are rarely easy or beautiful. The difficult moments crack us open, though we struggle against this. I hope that in my own vulnerable moments I made the right choices. If so, that has itself. If not, at least there is the truth with nothing to hide behind.

And when we are cracked, we finally see
who is good,
who to trust,
who will love us despite our mistakes.

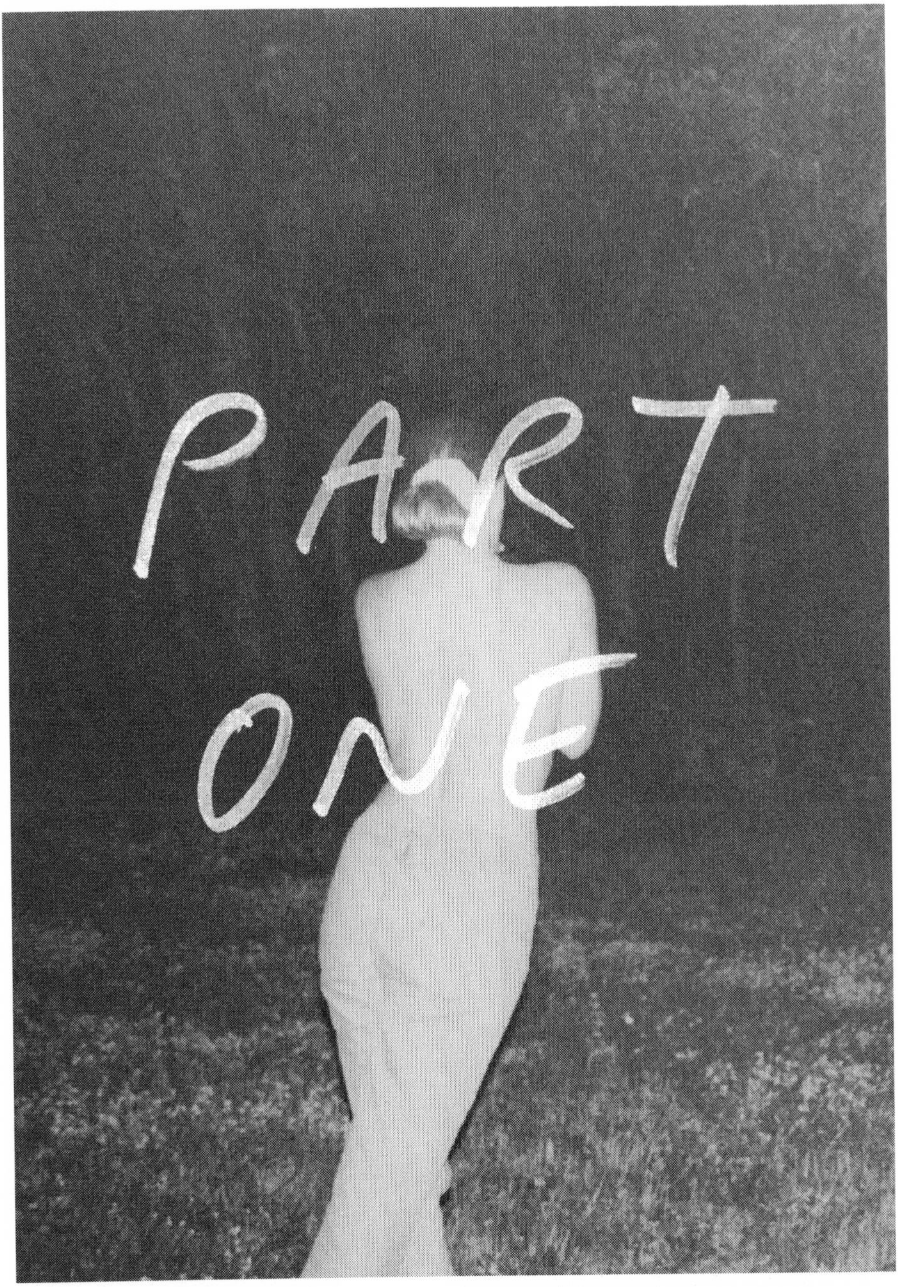
PART
ONE

I: The Body

Dear child, I only did to you what the sparrow
did to you; I am old when it is fashionable to be
young; I cry when it is fashionable to laugh.
I hated you when it would have taken less courage
to love.

Charles Bukowski

To Lyla, Given Up For Adoption

When your birth mother
was a baby,
her neck pulsed a furious heartbeat in the right side,
working and working without tire.
And now she sleeps
preparing for you, her eyes
dark and heavily lidded,
tired by late pregnancy in
her own childhood, her arms
crossed across her taut belly,
and you curled inside her,
kicking her from within,
waiting to be born.

Who are you,
little frond we will hand away?
You who we barely know,
whose breakfast face
whose nighttime fears
will be tended to by other hands.
The dimples on your knuckles
wet from teething.
What will your cry sound like?
The small smell of your neck,
each of your fingers,
that sound of breath
between each sucking of milk,
your eyes soft in pleasure.
I miss you already.

We will soon hand you over
to the sturdily good.
Survivors, soul predecessors
of our stock, hand you over
to those to whom God
first spoke in the desert.
You'll speak their language first,

knowing the names of the sons
who spread east to Canaan to multiply.
And you, a daughter. The dust of the earth.
How will you speak to us from all that?

If after a year or ten you hear
the Elgar or a soft Bach
from a neighbor's open window,
the salt of the Pacific
tangled in your hair,
two thousand miles from us,
will you lift your face to wonder where you heard it before?
You surely remember, from when you formed, from frond to bone,
inside your too-young mother
who played a French cello beside the window
as spring quite suddenly cast its first bloom
on the hawthorne
your great grandfather planted
fifty years before your birth.

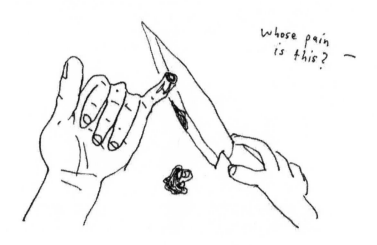

whose pain
is this? —

disaster

Tuesday, November 8th, 2016

I had burned the fingers of my left hand cooking something
my neoconservative brother would have dismissed as vegan shit,
pulling a bubbling cast iron skillet from the oven.
Ramon stood behind me, rolling a clove between
his brown cheek and bottom teeth, talking of his mother:
"this pan, my mother, she used. She used to call it *su única arma*
since she wouldn't touch the guns on the farm."
He chewed the bulb of the herb, his fingers crushing
another into the mole sauce.
"She had lifted the skillet against my father once
when he came home after too much drink.
She had to use both hands (his eyes got big, fingers spreading).
My brother Miguel and I sat hiding under the sturdy of the kitchen
table.
I saw her feet facing his, and he went to bed soon after,
defeated. It was never talked about again."
I looked down. My own pan was Ozark kin, cast off to my little liberal
Pueblo-colored kitchen after a decade of neglect on the wood burning
stove.
It cooks chocolate and chilies 202 miles from the fields
where I grew up. It has never seen violence.

At my dinner table, not a single one of us could eat.
We sat together, two women, two people of color, Ramon
and his thin lover, whose waist I always admired,
holding hands on top of the table, safely.
And we were hopeful. We opened bottles of wine,
the dogs lay panting at our feet
while our children made happy noise from the other room.
I pictured our whole future, I pictured the quiet delight of
visiting family overseas, proud of America
with first a person of color and then a female president.
I liked our candidate. I liked the picture
of her in the dark sunglasses best,
the way age sat on her face.

We were confident as the sun was setting.
Someone got out the good bourbon. Poured it over ice.
My long dead grandfather would have cringed, he drank it neat.
(When I looked over at you across the room, you, my lover, always
the quietest one, who wanted the quiet always,
smiling through our noise, all the daylight sadness was gone from your
face.)
I was giddy. Giddy like Six Flags when you're young
and finally tall enough for roller coasters.
Losing your virginity to a good boy giddy.
Good new president giddy, the way I felt
when I was pregnant and thought, maybe just maybe
I would switch to a female OBGYN, shocking my mother,
but some sort of adolescent courage steered me.
No. A woman is going to pull this baby girl from between my legs.
And tonight, a mom was going to be president.

Later then, after Michigan, and then Pennsylvania,
we left the dishes and picked up the small heavy bodies of our children
who had fallen asleep on the floor with their books between them.
"Sólo quiero estar acostado y no pensar," Ramon almost whispered,
and we opened the windows to the cold night.

Remember when Sugar Ray Robinson lost in 1951?
His barrel of a chest, the smooth bridge of his nose.
I wasn't born yet, but my grandfather talked about it,
had newspaper clippings of his fall caught mid-air
in his top dresser drawer, the one we couldn't reach.
The one that kept the handgun.
He said men turned off the television that night so they didn't see his
great body fall to the slight bounce of the ring.

I thought of that referee, his knees next to the great head of Robinson
as I washed my blistering ring finger, the dishes soaking.
I ran it under cold water, watching the pink skin buckle a bit.
I put it in my mouth.
as though to suck out all of the pain.

Car Crash

There's a man in a yellow vest sweeping shards of chrome,
fragments of glass, and one large bumper
from the center of Highway 141 during morning
rush-hour traffic.

His industrial-grade broom moves between twisted cars
like he's dancing it between couples.
There's no sign of distress on his face.
His lips purse in quiet whistle in his work.
He sees death every day. It's just his job.

The cars in the one open lane
inch around him, the mouths of the drivers
changing from frustration to concern
as we see our faces reflected in the
crumpled steel, the blood left over
on the concrete, staining the mirrored twists
of the bumper broken off the sedan that sits motionless, cold,
windows busted out, one car door still open, ignored,
the last of the smoke still creeping from under the hood.

This man, you've passed him one hundred times.
He has stood one lane over at the gas station,
perhaps in front of you
in the line for a hotdog at Busch Stadium.
He has been near you, in the line at the grocer.
He even held the door for you once.

Neck

There's something inside my neck.
Right side, below my ear,
when you put your finger to it
there is a pulse.
And a bump. Bigger than the left side.
Firm.
Last month I took my lover's hand and asked him (you know that
moment when you're done with the kissing and the washing up)
"do you feel that?" taking his hand, his skin still warm
from before, to the spot.
His brow paused suddenly,
he looked up at the ceiling like he was considering
if there would be rain and said,
"it's nothing."
He went back to tying his shoes, checked his watch,
and kissed me goodbye.

Next steps.
Tonight I showed
my mother, whose face
was more stern, with
all the weight of funerals in it.
Pressing around, caring enough to push and turn my face,
she drew her weathered face closer,
and pulling away
she smiled, relieved.
"It's nothing," she said.
Then kissed, too wet,
my forehead, settling in next to me.

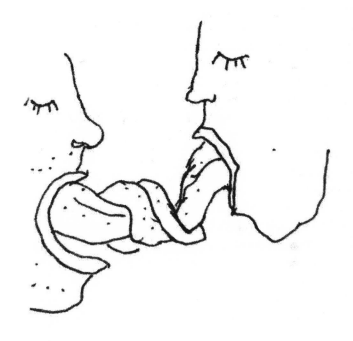

Calling You To End It

Go feel good, I say,
my ear pressing the phone against my shoulder.
I don't have time to read Vonnegut,
and you have been so hungry for so long.

A girl wants something darker than
the clean lines of French,
the oyster knife's silver
brightness above her lap on a Provence Sunday.

I need the black Sicilian beach.
The oil from centuries-old volcano.
The firm brown belly of the local man and his chilies.
It's not personal.

Montmartre

At Sacré-Cœur before the final bells,
I prayed hard to find you.
I had climbed the steps,
and beneath my necklace's silver icon
I reached for your cold fingers,
but you were quiet.
Sign of the cross, sign of the cross
hearing the strange Latin,
the blood on the cross, the tears of the saints,
their frozen eyes raised to the fresco ceiling.

The confessional line was too long,
so when the priest called, "*devoted ones,* it is time to go,"
I listed my sins quickly against my skin,
one long fingernail dragging the length
of the words *I'm sorry I am very sorry* on my thigh
under the pulling stitch of the tights,
the wool fabric of my skirt.

The women stood all of them at once in their sturdy shoes,
square in torso and sides, dotting from their pews
and walking wordlessly to rue Caulaincourt.
So I stood too, *time to leave it's time,*
leaving the church to the cold feet of
beggars, their cardboard peppered with trinkets
of the God who never wrote me back.

The priest pushed closed the heavy doors
to walk back to his single glass of red wine and coarse
brown blanket. And walking home to my one room
I realized how hungry I was, how hungry I've always been,
sitting still in Catholic school *shhh,* sitting with knees together *shhh*
straightening the grey uniform with my fingers.

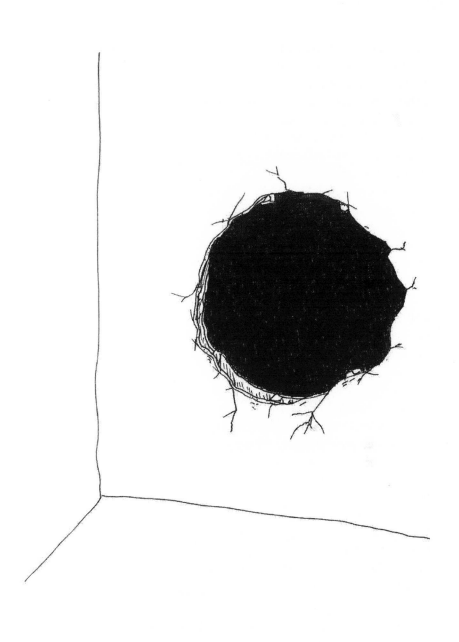

Five, Skinny

My mother worked at a bookstore
in the shopping mall.
She brought home castaway paperbacks,
their covers torn off by the boss,
their yellowing pages dog eared.
And she read them with a bourbon
in the middle of the night, waiting on the nights
my father didn't come home.

Some evenings she'd let me comb her hair,
my thin child's fingers long against her scalp,
the brown tendrils matching my own,
their length between my fingers,
her mind far off to his body in other women's beds,
their strange bodies to be somehow brought home to her
at the witching hour.

Standing those years in the store gave my mom
lines of spider veins whose maps
I would trace with my finger
as I sat between her feet in church.

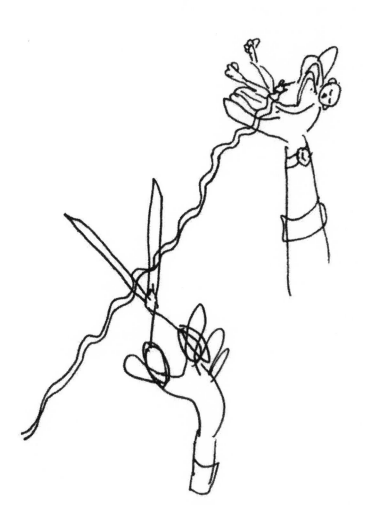

Dear Baby

Dear baby who is crippling my own,
low left sciatica baby
dawn sick water baby
belly cramp in the deep baby
tailbone fracturing baby
perineum splitting of a girl baby:

While you were busy being born, your mother,
her once tiny waist, lay smallish in the bed,
her blood pressure dropping
twenty two hours into her labor.
It was 3:00 AM and I was alone at her feet, rubbing, kneading.
The alarms going off, the nurses in scrubs rushed in,
and I thought you should know
I thought of how I might make myself die soon after.
I knew I would if anything
happened to that girl.
Here's what I remember:

Years ago when my hair was a heavy braid down my back there was a boy
who would come to the hall down the street from our gravel road. He
was not handsome. He would dance with every girl. His feet moved so
fast he seemed to blur, all the height of him moving by the stage where
the man who sang combed his hair in between every song, the lines of
tonic neat in the barn lights. One night I snuck out to meet him. I
dressed silently at as everyone else slept, a Kent stolen from my mother's
purse (for the walk to the hall). Before though, I stood in a slip with my
hair in curlers and looked at the small line of clothes in my closet and
chose the skirt that would look best with his arm circling my waist.
When I was that age I didn't know that one day I'd sit rubbing the feet of
my daughter giving birth to you, her heart in trouble.

In a northern Missouri college town there's a house on South Franklin I'd
pass when walking home from the library late at night. The house had
been boarded up for ten years, no one inside. I'd always make the sign of
the cross when walking past since sometimes there was a shadow in the
window on the third floor and a person there reading in low light.

It feels good to light a match, to push your hand deep into a good glove.
There are things that don't feel good too.
One day the girls' pet fish fell into the dish disposal and I had to
put my hand deep into the hole to cup his damp floundering.
But he lived. My husband's hand was too big, and he just looked at me,
expecting me to let it die. But I did reach in.
I do like the earthy smell of the slouching puppy
lifted from his cedar warmth.
Like your body, from my daughter's.
I think of you now born.
And the girl's heart turned out alright,
and I tell myself
I should write a poem about that too.

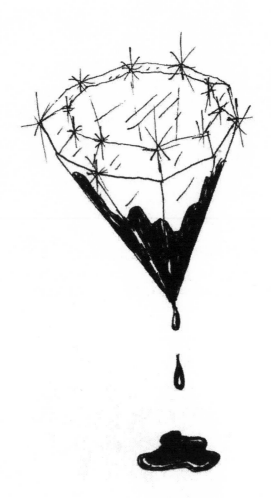

Abstract Sleep

He wiped his sweating brow,
leaning in to hear my response,
his face beaked in concentration.

Men walk each step a cold wince
as you're breaking apart forms while
working the gearshift from the tractor's sticking bustle.
The way fonts go in and out of style?
The black corner lipstick of a beagle.
Once everything is over,
you realize not thinking was the sweetness.

When we were young, we simply weren't watched.
The welders in the garage:
("Don't look at the light," my father said,
his welding wand sparking
a horsehair crest about his helmet,
arcs of fear that still pull at my entrails).

We are Midwestern people,
so we have to work to remember the names of the artists in the museum.
We only know the live oak forests with a black dog's company,
chickens that eat the ticks.
And no matter how much you love that one sweet hen,
the slow one who never lays,
it's not like the children's books say. If she doesn't lay the eggs
she's Sunday dinner, and you're not allowed to cry about it
if you don't want the part that happens when you cry.
And bird dogs,
(Will you stay here till I fall asleep?)
the way they look in the fields since it's in their sinews
when the shadows are long and cool and the light is still warm,
the painter's hour.

I thought this morning about the courage to love,
and it hit me suddenly, all these cars
on the road right next to us and what if everyone

has panic. All of us, together apart?
Here's the thing:
There won't ever be love again.
And what do you have to say to that?
(You left the only man who ever loved you, asshole. You don't deserve
another chance.
You have the ghosts to keep you company).

I like to stand outside your front windows best.
You don't close those shades.
And I see your book on its side and the stacks of papers and
the cold cup of coffee you abandoned.
You've stopped drinking. Don't you miss those cups of wine?
Do you know who you want waiting for you when you die?

I cleaned around the plants today.
Things had crawled out of them to find bigger things.
They died from impact.
When the cactus cut my finger
I started to look at the inside of it until the blood pooled below
and the dog lapped at it.

I know some time must have passed
since the scab is here now. The cut has all grown out.
It took about as long as it did for you to be quiet from my mind.
We let the things we should take care of just slide away.

When the baby was little, once I got locked out of the house.
I knocked on Mrs. Feldt's door, she was the German across the street
we all were afraid of. I was desperate. I had to borrow her phone.
The baby needed her bottle and was fussing.
I had never knocked before. Her sparse furniture
and the story the neighbors whispered about (the day
her husband died in front of her) kept me away.
Watching from her curtains, she let me in after a too-long moment of
knocking,
and as the baby cried, her back arching in hunger,
the woman reached for her.

I didn't give the baby over.

I held her to my breast.

Later, my husband asked, "Why? She is old. And lonely."

I didn't tell him I had worried. I didn't want her running down the hall and locking the door.

And I said no.

God.

I said no.

Westhampton Lake

Westhampton Lake sat brooding, two hundred feet
from our dusty yard. Its wet face was silent.
But the water, our fathers said, was deep,
and we were forbidden from wading in.

One summer afternoon a snapping turtle
made his way from the water, prehistoric in his spiny ridges.
Too big to hide in his shell, his long neck growled
as the dogs circled him, keeping their distance.
What did he seek in our yard? He darted
behind the snowplow resting in the tall grass,
digging in the rustling chains.

My brothers picked him up by the tail, and in the
the bed of the truck, I inched one yellow pencil
close to his face, until his jaws, like a man's,
snapped the pencil into a splintery half.
My father, home later, backed the Chevy down to the water,
which seemed to be waiting, to deposit the
turtle back to the cold mud.

The next day I found the eggs, mostly buried
behind the yard's machines. Perfect circles,
whiter than the chicken's, these little lives.
She had left the lake with her babies
only for us to force her back. I could imagine her
body, released by my father's gloved hands,
a shadow under the dark water,
her broad nostrils skimming the surface for air.

I pulled the eggs from the crumbly earth,
just barely larger than the bluejay's and rounder,
then barefoot, with their tiny bodies tucked into my shirt
lifted to show a pale abdomen where one day
my own children would grow, one to live,
one to die inside of me. I walked them

to the mossy edge of Westhampton for their
nighthatch, whispering into the dark to their mother.

II: The Spirit

I want you to come to me without a past.
Those lines you've learned, forget them.
Forget that you've been here before in other bedrooms in other places.
Come to me new.
Never say you love me until that day when you have proved it.

Jeanette Winterson

The Windows in Winter

January is the cold month without holiday, the quarter inch
of dry snow, dirt-packed in the corners of the window,
the yard a garden of salt one foot from where we sleep.
We fall back and forth against each other's
warm spines, the breath between us, our feet
touching, your skin almost earth damp.

4:00 AM is what the occultus knew. The witching hour
when the bodies all tiptoe down the hall to me,
my body held down again, darkness creeping in like the cold,
dizzy under their longish hands, and you asleep.

Love is the small goodness. Your voice heavy
from sleep on my collarbone, paint between
your middle and ring fingers reaching, your hand
pulling that warm space at my navel
against your chest. It is the mouth, the clear run
under your lip I tasted. Your face in the dark,
shooing off the creature on the hearth with your broom.

In spring I'll wear a kerchief like my grandmother did
and take a rag to those window corners,
wiping away the winter, the funerals, the change of seasons.
(The one who canned fruit in the space under the stairs.
Dirt floor, damp in the autumn, I followed her close,
fingers in her apron strings, her generous bosom just above,
the skin of her hand a papery cream,
sliding the cap onto mason jars, blues and purples like blood,
all settled).

Since February

I learned how men love on a farm in central Missouri.
My father taught me, to know always
what direction I was facing.
His hands on my shoulders, maybe one
covering my eyes, my child's nose too,
he turned my body around and around in test,
on the endless lakes, even in the dusty fields,
the smell of gasoline from the tractor on his hands,
coarse from small male labors, and behind us
the birds' sturdy landing in the quiet wake.

Girls growing up chase the black dogs
chasing deer, but then it happens almost overnight.
At twelve or so, the flocks in their dawn water
become a little lonely. Men begin to look different,
stepping between logs becomes purposeful,
and we walk with caution into deeper water.
And now, I bend to roll my pants
for the wading into you.

It was warm this February,
some random Sunday I shudder to think
I nearly passed over
because of all the reading.
But I quickly finished my coffee and walked to meet you.
You were suddenly there; you stood facing east on Grand Avenue
with your hands in your pockets, with your height
and your eyes far off and your shirt holding the shape
of your shoulders.

Since February I've started running my hands
along the wood of the desk,
smooth under my book in the library,
the lines in the wood invisible before you.
Now though, there's the matter of your body
moving through your day.
Your hands, the fingers around the things

you carry, then after, around my waist, my face.
And so
the wood requires
touch.

Dutchtown in Spring

Every winter the cold ground pins brown to green,
all fronds having crawled six feet under,
all silence save the wind,
and the crocus and locust wait under the frost.
Even the fox's feet are quiet through the frozen grass.
He has surprised me in your backyard,
that feral face stone cold in the dirt. He's waiting too,
how long we all wait before spring,
until April's cruel rain.

The windows fog with our morning breath.
Walking for coffee, the dogs between your moving feet,
your hands peeling an orange, the scent of it
on your fingers after.
Bluegrass on the ratio interrupting your breath
on my collarbone and there is nothing ahead in the day.

Sometimes the chords change
(first to the perfect fifth) in a song,
and I look up and believe.

Early Summer Clay Pigeons

June's heat pins green to brown in the south field, the fronds
crawling out from waisthigh buffalo grass.
The shotgun stirs the sudden cries of greyfurred animals
into the fields, the locust song from under canna lilies early shoots,
his abdomen curled in the heat, cupped in the half-rot of spring.

The brown barrel rests in your hand, and you're saying something,
but I cannot hear save the echo of the gun's cracking inside my chest.
Your hands cradle shells, and I am more afraid of what
loving you could do to me than what any bullet might.

Mostly now, you're in the space where I move my chest
to button my blouse, my lips as I line them in red before work.
In the steam from the spoon I blow on before dinner,
my arm as I reach behind to unzip my dress at the end of the day.

Last night I stood in the rain walking the dogs.
I felt the wet, warm this time of year between
my shirt and skin, suddenly soaked with it,
and I thought of how wanting you
feels like love at sixteen and the best song plays
on the radio and you're driving
and the car is full of people who cry out and
what if I could tell myself, younger, that there would be these moments,
your arm around me at a range in the slanting light of afternoon,
your kiss later on a gun's bruise on my shoulder,
hands reaching with coffee, the sweet aching
of not being ever close enough.
How do I press this moment into something I won't break apart?

If I could build the perfect night, we could watch
the stars come out one by one, our sides together.
The length of your finger raised, naming each one.

The Oils

Picasso painted profiles and frontals
of the women he passed on the Mougins cobblestones.
He took his time walking in the mornings
the long way to the French pool.
He believed swimming kept a man strong in body
and in bedroom.

He was pleased by the way their navy skirts
grazed the backs of their knees,
the fabric rustling as they walked expertly with
cigarette, with parcel, with short heels
covering the slopes of their feet.

Every day he rose early, pulling the cotton shirt over
his face, a canvas in his mind. Walking,
he parted the street conversations,
all their strange angles, with knees closely crossed, knees
he couldn't touch under tables of coffee, their cheeks
he might kiss, one, two, then back, but whose sharp
corners were not his until, finally, under stretched canvas,
the powdered pigment crusted under his nail beds,
in the browned-creased corners of his eyes,
their bodies became grotesque and real,
his *demoiselle* squatting in oils.

I wonder if he paused after passing someone
extraordinary. A woman whose waist was like mother
like child, like lover all wrapped together.
She would be French confident. Perhaps he would turn
back to catch a second glimpse before she rounded the corner,
forever gone.
He could maybe smell the lilac perfume she lifted
to her jawbone that morning,
and taking that back to his plaster
with the fourteen blues of his palette
like one who has found
a bloom to place into his book.

First found, then into the sensible wool of his pocket for later,
cradled like a small bird to be pressed
carefully under film.

It's as if I have passed you on the street
seeing the pleasing angle
of your jaw, the creased-corners
of your light eyes. And the startling upon
looking back, I see you've turned back too.

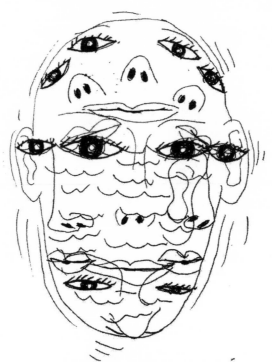

NOT A TIBETAN BUDDHIST PAINTING.

Second Date

Inching towards you is
our knees
bumping under the table
and it feeling nice.
It's you ordering after I do,
asking to share a cup of soup
instead of having your own.
It's hearing your voice say
your dog's nickname
(I'm suddenly witness to this morning affection of yours).
It's asking to hold my hand
driving through Muir Woods,
just to see how it feels.

Stepping back from you is
the framed photograph of you
with your lover
twelve inches from the couch where
your left hand holds
my thigh.
It's the lines of your vacuumed car rug because you're
moving thousands of miles away.
It's that we can't yet walk down the street, your hand
low on my back
to steer our course.
You love someone else.

That plunge in the heart.
You have appeared quite suddenly
with your height,
your hand on the steering wheel,
your skin and your mouth,
suddenly no longer simply not here.
Now somehow reminding me of
the details women imagine
at thirteen, how men may one day look at us,
how they may smell, how when

they stand behind us in the doorway,
like you did in the dark, listening to our friend
read his poems. How we must
be able to feel the warm from under their clothes,
though we do not yet touch.

NOT PORN

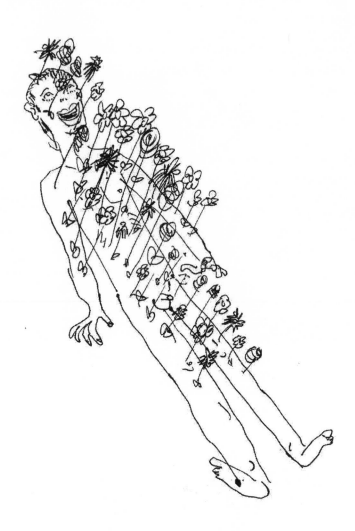

California

We had one day.
He drove us all the way to Muir Woods.
The roads climbed and the trees were silent.
We ate crab and drank beer in the sun,
and my chest sunburned.

We had three hours while the rest of the party
walked to Castro, the flags in the strong cool wind,
the flags and faces of homes I skipped to
draw out this one afternoon a little longer.
I told him I would need a bourbon for what we were about to do.
Without the courage of other women,
I walked close next to him to the bar next to the library
while the sun was still high in the sky.

We worked the crossword in bed until
the ice against my lips burned away my fear.
The windows were open to the view of the brick,
the sounds of the street below some
strange voyeur.

There were Japanese businessmen in the next room.
The windows had been open.
We all shared an elevator on the way down to the lobby,
and one turned to look quickly at me,
his head bowed.
Later, the children asked, does the burn hurt?

sans

suici

One Month

In December there are thirty-one days.
Days people are born into, days
that take bodies from us (where do they go?).
In one month we really don't know a thing
about anybody.

I want to speak about how love is not too far
from the matter of country water,
of birds landing on it, the quiet wake
their sturdy bodies make at dawn, far away
from city lights, and how when growing up
a girl in the country, a flock landing in water is
a little lonely. The rural poor know the
the long days of work ahead, and if a woman is lucky,
she will grow to stack her own wood at the stove
next to the body of someone strong,
her heart dressed in its Sunday best
with December's wind against the window.

Last night was the smallest thing.
You came in from the night cold, snow dusting
the bulk of your jacket, the paper bag in your arms,
bread, buttercream, tomatoes. I thought, as you moved
your hands taking out the dinner, your mouth moving,
you must have been fair-haired in your childhood.
When you were little, you told me, you had church
in place of my fields, all the wrong kind of God
shoved into you.

Later, on the bed, the cover worn from
years of the crawling children and their puppies
and books whose dust left stains I looked at with just my own eyes,
because no one else has ever,
ever, in years (after years in the same bed facing the same direction)
now the second half of life approaching), sat
while the wind pushed hard against the window.
You slept hard, your body transfixed by dreams, rising chest,

my palm against the smooth run of your brow in
the still morning next to you, like that greenblue lake
filling the whole sky of the bedroom.

lets die

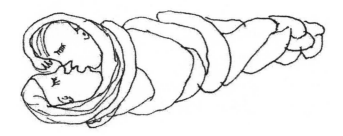

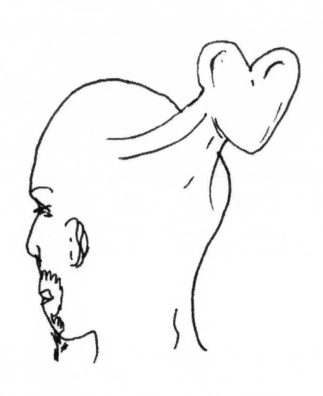

Westhampton Lake II

Summer:
Westhampton Lake sat in the heat, our tractor circling its wet face.
I sat behind my brother, my right arm around his belly,
listening to the cylinders of the engine whose sound I remembered
thirty years from that lake when I steered the Chevy
into an aching turn, too low in gear.
The dark mouth of the road stirred my sleeping daughter,
a sunburn in the part of her black hair.

Those yellow afternoons of AM radio were the beagles
Tic-Tac and his black-headed son Bluff
hiding from the heat under the truck, were the tractor's slow
pace in ground speed, was my brother's squinting at the sun,
lifting his hat off his head, wiping his brow, then leaning back
into the work and the feeling of the nooks in the earth below the wheels
and the ending afternoon light meant we could have dinner soon.
The girls all wondered if we would ever know a man
not father, not brother.

We learn first love through these small trusts:
The brothers keeping you safe, their hands pulling yours
tight around their body on the tractor's perch, the small command of
hold tight. Their eyes aiming at the neighborhood boys' faces, warning
them away. We take for granted the dogs will be safe,
the female darting too close to the wheels, her nose locked to a trail
circling the bluegreen perimeter of the lake.
She would touch her paw to the mossy edge, only to pull it back again,
which I would do that evening, barefoot, watching the boys
wading in with wincing laughter, all the childhood courage
in their long abdomens, their sneakers on the side
of the sandy shore.

Winter:
Two nights ago, no moon in the icy sky, he came to me soaked,
his chest naked under his coat after the factory shift.
I lifted the coat from his arms, our freckled shoulders matching
as winter pushed hard against the windows.

He bent to unlace the boots, his spine a pearled ripple under skin,
and my body suddenly ached back,
to have had childhood with him, to funnel backwards,
to put my arms around this one's body on the tractor
in the tall grass, the crickets' arching jumps
in the afternoon slant of light.

In the winter, Westhampton Lake froze.
Alone one grey morning, I snuck out
(two children had drowned when they cracked through the ice
a generation before),
and with my breath leading, too young to care about dying,
I threw stones to test its weight. I listened for the groaning crack.
And in a still moment of courage, I walked. First slowly,
watching the icy veins below, then faster
above solid crystal, clear through, holding my weight
over the quiet ice.

Summer:
Decades from that still water, and alone in adulthood at the lake,
I am the one steering. I am suddenly the Love,
all of it, a sweet weight on me I can't imagine not bearing
as I lift the girl's body, heavy with sleep, and her arms,
browned by a day in the sun, reach around my neck
as I close the heavy door behind me with my boot.

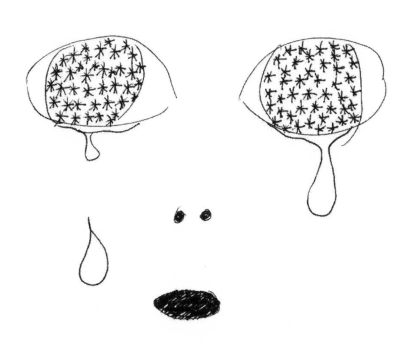

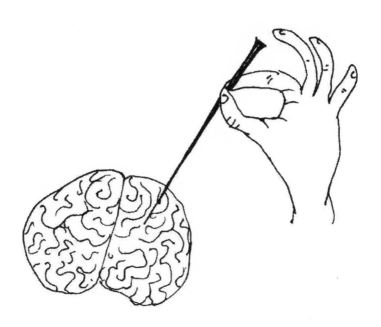

NOTES

Allison Cundiff is an adjunct Professor of English at Lindenwood University and an English teacher at Parkway North High School. Her publications include two books of poetry, *Otherings* (2016, Golden Antelope Press), and *In Short, A Memory of the Other on a Good Day,* co-authored with Steven Schreiner, (2014, Golden Antelope Press) articles in *The Pragmatic Buddhist, The St. Louis Post Dispatch, Feminist Teacher,* fiction in *In Layman's Terms,* and poetry in *The Chariton Review.* She lives in St. Louis.

Anthony Gaddis is an artist & filmmaker based in Los Angeles, California. www.anthonygaddis.com

Made in the USA
Columbia, SC
24 May 2018